From:

Date:

A Mother's Guide

TO THE TEN COMMANDMENTS

The quoted ideas expressed in this book (but not Scripture verses) are not, in all cases, exact quotations, as some have been edited for clarity and brevity. In all cases, the author has attempted to maintain the speaker's original intent. In some cases, quoted material for this book was obtained from secondary sources, primarily print media. While every effort was made to ensure the accuracy of these sources, the accuracy cannot be guaranteed. For additions, deletions, corrections, or clarifications in future editions of this text, please write Freeman-Smith, LLC.

Scripture quotations are taken from:

The Holy Bible, King James Version

The Holy Bible, New International Version (NIV) Copyright © 1973, 1978, 1984, by International Bible Society. Used by permission of Zondervan Publishing House. All rights reserved.

The Holy Bible, New King James Version (NKJV) Copyright © 1982 by Thomas Nelson, Inc. Used by permission.

The New American Standard Bible®, (NASB) Copyright © 1960, 1962, 1963, 1968, 1971, 1972, 1973, 1975, 1977, 1995 by The Lockman Foundation. Used by permission.

Holy Bible, New Living Translation, (NLT) Copyright © 1996. Used by permission of Tyndale House Publishers, Inc., Wheaton, Illinois 60189. All rights reserved.

The Message (MSG)- This edition issued by contractual arrangement with NavPress, a division of The Navigators, U.S.A. Originally published by NavPress in English as THE MESSAGE: The Bible in Contemporary Language copyright 2002-2003 by Eugene Peterson. All rights reserved.

International Children's Bible®, New Century Version®. (ICB) Copyright © 1986, 1988, 1999 by Tommy Nelson™, a division of Thomas Nelson, Inc. All rights reserved. Used by permission.

New Century Version®. (NCV) Copyright © 1987, 1988, 1991 by Word Publishing, a division of Thomas Nelson, Inc. All rights reserved. Used by permission.

The Holman Christian Standard Bible™ (Holman CSB) Copyright © 1999, 2000, 2001 by Holman Bible Publishers. Used by permission.

Cover Design and Page Layout by Bart Dawson

ISBN 1-58334-322-9

Printed in the United States of America

A Mother's Guide

TO THE **TEN COMMANDMENTS**

TABLE OF CONTENTS

INTRODUCTION

Okay, Mom, here's a question for you: When was the last time you gave much thought to the Ten Commandments? Are you one of those women who can recite the Ten Commandments in order and without error, or can you recall only six or seven commandments as you rack your brain fruitlessly for the rest?

If you're like many women who grew up in the church, you most certainly could recite the Ten Commandments by heart when you were a young girl. But those days may be long gone. If so, this text can serve as a refresher course on the relevance that the Ten Commandments should play in your own life and in the lives of your family members.

God gave us His commandments so that we might obey them and be blessed. Corrie ten Boom observed, "Perfect obedience would be perfect happiness, if only we had perfect confidence in the power we were obeying." Her words remind us that when we obey God, we are rewarded. But, we live in a world that presents us with countless temptations to stray far from God's path. We Christians, when confronted with sin, have clear instructions: We must walk—or better yet run—in the opposite direction.

For the next 31 days, the devotional readings in this text will challenge you to consider the role that the Ten Commandments plays in your life—and, more importantly, the role that these commandments should play in your life. The Ten Commandments have served as a shining beacon for Christians of every generation. May you, as a thoughtful Christian mother, be mindful of God's laws, and may you apply them to your life today and always.

THE TEN COMMANDMENTS

And God spoke all these words, saying: "I am the Lord your God, who brought you out of the land of Egypt, out of the house of bondage. You shall have no other gods before Me. You shall not make for yourself a carved image, or any likeness of anything that is in heaven above, or that is in the earth beneath, or that is in the water under the earth; you shall not bow down to them nor serve them. For I, the Lord your God, am a jealous God, visiting the iniquity of the fathers on the children to the third and fourth generations of those who hate Me, but showing mercy to thousands, to those who love Me and keep My commandments. You shall not take the name of the Lord your God in vain, for the Lord will not hold him guiltless who takes His name in vain. Remember the Sabbath day, to keep it holy. Six days you shall labor and do all your work, but the seventh day is the Sabbath of the Lord your God. In it you shall do no work: you, nor your son, nor your daughter, nor your male servant, nor your female servant, nor your cattle, nor your stranger who is within your gates. For in six days the Lord made the heavens and the earth, the sea, and all that is in them, and rested the seventh day. Therefore the Lord blessed the

Sabbath day and hallowed it. Honor your father and your mother, that your days may be long upon the land which the Lord your God is giving you. You shall not murder. You shall not commit adultery. You shall not steal. You shall not bear false witness against your neighbor. You shall not covet your neighbor's house; you shall not covet your neighbor's wife, nor his male servant, nor his female servant, nor his ox, nor his donkey, nor anything that is your neighbor's."

Exodus 20:1-17 NKJV

THE FIRST COMMANDMENT:

NO OTHER GODS

The First Commandment states: "You shall have no other gods before Me."

God makes it clear that you must worship Him and Him alone. During the next three days, think about your need to place God first in your own life and in the collective life of your family.

CHAPTER 1

GOD FIRST

Jesus answered and said unto him,
If a man love me, he will keep my words:
and my Father will love him, and we will come
unto him, and make our abode with him.

John 14:23 KJV

I n Exodus 20:3, God makes it clear that we must have no other gods before Him. Yet the world tempts us to do otherwise. The world is a noisy, distracting place, a place that offers countless temptations and dangers. The world seems to cry, "Worship me with your time, your money, your energy, your thoughts, and your life!" But if we are wise, we won't fall prey to that temptation.

As you think about the nature of your relationship with God, remember this: you will always have some type of relationship with Him—it is inevitable that your life must be lived in relationship to God. The question is not if you will have a relationship with Him; the burning question is whether or not that relationship will be one that seeks to honor Him . . . or not.

Are you willing to place God first in your life? And, are you willing to welcome God's Son into your heart? Unless you can honestly answer these questions with a resounding yes, then your relationship with God isn't what it could be or should be. Thankfully, God is always available, He's always ready to forgive, and He's waiting to hear from you now. The rest, of course, is up to you.

Make God's will the focus of your life day by day.
If you seek to please Him and Him alone,
you'll find yourself satisfied with life.

Kay Arthur

To yield to God means to belong to God, and to
belong to God means to have all His infinite power.
To belong to God means to have all.

Hannah Whitall Smith

Don't worry about what you do not understand.
Worry about what you do understand
in the Bible but do not live by.

Corrie ten Boom

Don't be addicted to approval. Follow your heart.
Do what you believe God is telling you to do,
and stand firm in Him and Him alone.

Joyce Meyer

Happy are those who fear the Lord. Yes, happy are those who delight in doing what he commands.

Psalm 112:1 NLT

For this is the love of God, that we keep his commandments . . . .

1 John 5:3 KJV

Whoso despiseth the word shall be destroyed: but he that feareth the commandment shall be rewarded.

Proverbs 13:13 KJV

TODAY'S TIP:

Is He first in your family? Every family puts something or someone in first place. Does God occupy first place in your family? If so, congratulations! If not, it's time to reorder your priorities.

CHAPTER 2

TRUST HIM

And God, in his mighty power, will protect you until you receive this salvation, because you are trusting him.
1 Peter 1:5 NLT

O pen your Bible to its center, and you'll find the Book of Psalms. In it are some of the most beautiful words ever translated into the English language, with none more beautiful than the 23rd Psalm. David describes God as being like a shepherd who cares for His flock. No wonder these verses have provided comfort and hope for generations of believers.

You are precious in the eyes of God. You are His priceless creation, made in His image, and protected by Him. God watches over every step you make and every breath you take, so you need never be afraid. But sometimes, fear has a way of slipping into the minds and hearts of even the most devout believers. You are no exception.

On occasion, you will confront circumstances that trouble you to the very core of your soul. When you are afraid, trust in God. When you are worried, turn your concerns over to Him. When you are anxious, be still and listen for the quiet assurance of God's promises. And then, place your life in His hands. He is your shepherd today and throughout eternity. Trust the Shepherd.

Trusting God does not make me less of a woman.
It doesn't compromise my personality as
a strong woman. Depending on Him celebrates the
wonderful, miraculous gift He has entrusted to me.
Trusting Him is my strength.

Suzanne Dale Ezell

I'm discovering that the first step toward a vital,
trusting relationship with God is speaking
the truth—bringing myself out of the shadows and
talking honestly to my Father.

Sheila Walsh

A major turning point in my life came when
I realized that being able to trust God is
grounded in staking the whole of my being on
the reality that he loves me.

Paula Rinehart

Let me encourage you to continue to wait with
faith. God may not perform a miracle,
but He is trustworthy to touch you and make you
whole where there used to be a hole.

Lisa Whelchel

For we walk by faith, not by sight.
2 Corinthians 5:7 NASB

*Do not let your hearts be troubled. Trust in God;
trust also in me. In my Father's house are many rooms;
if it were not so, I would have told you.
I am going there to prepare a place for you.*
John 14:1-2 NIV

*It is better to trust in the LORD than to put
confidence in man. It is better to trust in
the LORD than to put confidence in princes.*
Psalm 118:8-9 KJV

TODAY'S TIP:
In God we trust? You bet! One of the most important
lessons that you can ever learn is to trust God for
everything—not some things, not most things . . .
everything!

CHAPTER 3

PLEASE HIM FIRST

*For am I now trying to win the favor of people, or God?
Or am I striving to please people? If I were still trying
to please people, I would not be a slave of Christ.*

Galatians 1:10 Holman CSB

Are you a people-pleaser or a God-pleaser? Hopefully, you're far more concerned with pleasing God than you are with pleasing your friends. But face facts: even if you're a devoted Christian, you're still going to feel the urge to impress your friends and acquaintances—and sometimes that urge will be strong.

Peer pressure can be good or bad, depending upon who your peers are and how they behave. If your friends encourage you to follow God's will and to obey His commandments, then you'll experience positive peer pressure, and that's a good thing. But, if your friends encourage you to do foolish things, then you're facing a different kind of peer pressure . . . and you'd better beware.

To sum it up, here's your choice: you can choose to please God first, or you can fall victim to peer pressure. The choice is yours—and so are the consequences.

You will get untold flak for prioritizing God's
revealed and present will for your life over man's . . .
but, boy, is it worth it.

Beth Moore

True friends will always lift you higher and challenge
you to walk in a manner pleasing to our Lord.

Lisa Bevere

It is comfortable to know that we are responsible
to God and not to man. It is a small matter
to be judged of man's judgement.

Lottie Moon

If I had to advise parents, I should tell them to
take great care about the people with whom their
children associate. Much harm may result from bad
company, and we are inclined by nature to follow
the worse rather than the better.

St. Elizabeth Ann Seton

Stay away from a foolish man;
you will gain no knowledge from his speech.

Proverbs 14:7 Holman CSB

My son, if sinners entice you, don't be persuaded.

Proverbs 1:10 Holman CSB

Blessed is the man who walks not in the counsel of
the ungodly, nor stands in the path of sinners, nor sits in
the seat of the scornful; but his delight is in the law of
the Lord, and in His law he meditates day and night.

Psalm 1:1-2 NKJV

TODAY'S TIP:
Face facts: Since you can't please everybody, you're
better off trying to please God.

THE SECOND COMMANDMENT:

NO FALSE IMAGES

The Second Commandment states: "You shall not make for yourself a carved image, or any likeness of anything that is in heaven above, or that is in the earth beneath, or that is in the water under the earth; you shall not bow down to them nor serve them."

You live in a materialistic society. During the next four days, think about the images, the possessions, and the temptations that can lead you away from God—and then think about common-sense ways to resist these temptations.

CHAPTER 4

PRAISE HIM

I will praise You with my whole heart.
Psalm 138:1 NKJV

When is the best time to praise God? In church? Before dinner is served? When we tuck little children into bed? None of the above. The best time to praise God is all day, every day, to the greatest extent we can, with thanksgiving in our hearts and with a song on our lips.

Too many of us, even well-intentioned believers, tend to "compartmentalize" our waking hours into a few familiar categories: work, rest, play, family time, and worship. To do so is a mistake. Worship and praise should be woven into the fabric of everything we do; it should never be relegated to a weekly three-hour visit to church on Sunday morning.

Theologian Wayne Oates once admitted, "Many of my prayers are made with my eyes open. You see, it seems I'm always praying about something, and it's not always convenient—or safe—to close my eyes." Dr. Oates understood that God always hears our prayers and that the relative position of our eyelids is of no concern to Him.

Today, find a little more time to lift your concerns to God in prayer, and praise Him for all that He has done. Whether your eyes are open or closed, He's listening.

I am to praise God for all things, regardless of where they seem to originate. Doing this is the key to receiving the blessings of God.
Praise will wash away my resentments.

Catherine Marshall

Praise Him! Praise Him!
Tell of His excellent greatness.
Praise Him! Praise Him!
Ever in joyful song!

Fanny Crosby

Most of the verses written about praise in God's Word were voiced by people faced with crushing heartaches, injustice, treachery, slander, and scores of other difficult situations.

Joni Eareckson Tada

God is worthy of our praise and is pleased when we come before Him with thanksgiving.

Shirley Dobson

Is anyone happy? Let him sing songs of praise.
James 5:13 NIV

*Through Him then, let us continually offer up
a sacrifice of praise to God, that is,
the fruit of lips that give thanks to His name.*
Hebrews 13:15 NASB

*Praise ye the LORD. O give thanks unto the LORD;
for he is good: for his mercy endureth for ever.*
Psalm 106:1 KJV

TODAY'S TIP:
If you're a thoughtful believer, you'll make it a habit
to praise God many times each day, beginning with
your morning devotional.

CHAPTER 5

OBEY HIM

Those who obey his commands live in him,
and he in them. And this is how we know that
he lives in us: We know it by the Spirit he gave us.
1 John 3:24 NIV

How can we demonstrate our love for God? By accepting His Son as our personal Savior and by placing Christ squarely at the center of our lives and our hearts. Jesus said that if we are to love Him, we must obey His commandments (John 14:15). Thus, our obedience to the Master is an expression of our love for Him.

In Ephesians 2:10 we read, "For we are His workmanship, created in Christ Jesus for good works" (NKJV). These words are instructive: We are not saved by good works, but for good works. Good works are not the root, but rather the fruit of our salvation.

Today, let the fruits of your stewardship be a clear demonstration of your love for Christ. When you do, your good heart will bring forth many good things for yourself and for God. Christ has given you spiritual abundance and eternal life. You, in turn, owe Him good treasure from a single obedient heart: yours.

Obedience to God is our job.
The results of that obedience are God's.

Elisabeth Elliot

There is sharp necessity for giving Christ absolute
obedience. The devil bids for our complete self-will.
To whatever extent we give this self-will
the right to be master over our lives, we are,
to an extent, giving Satan a toehold.

Catherine Marshall

Obedience is a foundational stepping stone on
the path of God's Will.

Elizabeth George

God asked both Noah and Joshua to do something
unusual and difficult. They did it, and their
obedience brought them deliverance.

Mary Morrison Suggs

Here is my final advice:
Honor God and obey his commands.
Ecclesiastes 12:13 ICB

If they obey and serve him, they will spend the rest of
their days in prosperity and their years in contentment.
Job 36:11 NIV

For it is not those who hear the law who are righteous in
God's sight, but it is those who obey the law
who will be declared righteous.
Romans 2:13 NIV

TODAY'S TIP:

Obedience leads to spiritual growth: Anne Graham Lotz correctly observed, "If you want to discover your spiritual gifts, start obeying God. As you serve Him, you will find that He has given you the gifts that are necessary to follow through in obedience."

CHAPTER 6

KEEPING POSSESSIONS IN PERSPECTIVE

A pretentious, showy life is an empty life;
a plain and simple life is a full life.
Proverbs 13:7 MSG

How important are material possessions? Not as important as we might think. In the life of committed Christians, material possessions should play a rather small role. Of course, we all need the basic necessities of life, but once we meet those needs for ourselves and for our families, the piling up of possessions creates more problems than it solves. Our real riches, of course, are not of this world. We are never really rich until we are rich in spirit.

Martin Luther observed, "Many things I have tried to grasp and have lost. That which I have placed in God's hands I still have." His words apply to all of us. Our earthly riches are transitory; our spiritual riches are not.

Do you find yourself wrapped up in the concerns of the material world? If so, it's time to reorder your priorities by turning your thoughts and your prayers to more important matters. And, it's time to begin storing up riches that will endure throughout eternity: the spiritual kind.

When we put people before possessions in our hearts, we are sowing seeds of enduring satisfaction.

Beverly LaHaye

It's sobering to contemplate how much time, effort, sacrifice, compromise, and attention we give to acquiring and increasing our supply of something that is totally insignificant in eternity.

Anne Graham Lotz

The more we stuff ourselves with material pleasures, the less we seem to appreciate life.

Barbara Johnson

Therefore I tell you, do not worry about your life, what you will eat or drink; or about your body, what you will wear. Is not life more important than food, and the body more important than clothes? Look at the birds of the air;
they do not sow or reap or store away in barns,
and yet your heavenly Father feeds them.
Are you not much more valuable than they?
Matthew 6:25-26 NIV

Your heart will be where your treasure is.
Luke 12:34 NCV

Can your wealth or all [your] physical exertion
keep [you] from distress?
Job 36:19 Holman CSB

TODAY'S TIP:

Everything we have is on loan from God. Corrie ten Boom observed, "I have held many things in my hands, and I have lost them all; but whatever I have placed in God's hands, that I still possess." Remember: your real riches are in heaven, so conduct yourself accordingly . . . and teach your children to do likewise.

CHAPTER 7

THE TREASURE HUNT

Pure and undefiled religion before our God and Father is this: to look after orphans and widows in their distress and to keep oneself unstained by the world.

James 1:27 Holman CSB

All of mankind is engaged in a colossal, worldwide treasure hunt. Some people seek treasure from earthly sources, treasures such as material wealth or public acclaim; others seek God's treasures by making Him the cornerstone of their lives.

What kind of treasure hunter are you? Are you so caught up in the demands of everyday living that you sometimes allow the search for worldly treasures to become your primary focus? If so, it's time to reorganize your daily to-do list by placing God in His rightful place: first place. Don't allow anyone or anything to separate you from your Heavenly Father and His only begotten Son.

The world's treasures are difficult to find and difficult to keep; God's treasures are ever-present and everlasting. Which treasures, then, will you claim as your own?

I have a divided heart, trying to love God and the world at the same time. God says, "You can't love me as you should if you love this world too."

Mary Morrison Suggs

Consider seriously how quickly people change, and how little trust is to be had in them; and hold fast to God, who does not change.

St. Teresa of Avila

As we have by faith said no to sin, so we should by faith say yes to God and set our minds on things above, where Christ is seated in the heavenlies.

Vonette Bright

All those who look to draw their satisfaction from the wells of the world—pleasure, popularity, position, possessions, politics, power, prestige, finances, family, friends, fame, fortune, career, children, church, clubs, sports, sex, success, recognition, reputation, religion, education, entertainment, exercise, honors, health, hobbies—will soon be thirsty again!

Anne Graham Lotz

For whatever is born of God overcomes the world.
And this is the victory that has
overcome the world—our faith.

1 John 5:4 NKJV

Religion that God our Father accepts as pure
and faultless is this: to look after orphans and
widows in their distress and to keep oneself from
being polluted by the world.

James 1:27 NIV

If you lived on the world's terms, the world would love
you as one of its own. But since I picked you to
live on God's terms and no longer on
the world's terms, the world is going to hate you.

John 15:19 MSG

TODAY'S TIP:

Whose message? If you dwell on the world's message and you're setting yourself up for disaster. If you dwell on God's message, you're setting yourself up for victory.

THE THIRD COMMANDMENT:

TAKING THE LORD'S NAME IN VAIN

The Third Commandment warns, "You shall not take the name of the Lord your God in vain." These words serve as a powerful reminder that the words you choose to speak—and the spirit in which you choose to speak them—are important to God. During the next three days, think about the quality, the tone, and the content of your speech.

CHAPTER 8

THE WORDS YOU SPEAK

And you shall know the truth,
and the truth shall make you free.
John 8:32 NKJV

When God's spirit touches our hearts, we are confronted by a powerful force: the awesome, irresistible force of God's Truth. In response to that force, we will either follow God's lead (by allowing Him to guide our thoughts, our words, and our deeds), or we will resist God's calling (and accept the consequences of our rebellion).

Today, as you fulfill the responsibilities that God has placed before you, ask yourself this question: "Do my words and actions bear witness to the ultimate Truth that God has placed in my heart, or am I allowing the pressures of everyday life to overwhelm me?" It's a profound question that only you can answer.

The Bible clearly warns that you will be judged by the words you speak, so choose those words carefully. Very carefully.

To worship Him in truth means to worship Him
honestly, without hypocrisy, standing open
and transparent before Him.

Anne Graham Lotz

The Holy Spirit was given to guide us into all truth,
but He doesn't do it all at once.

Elisabeth Elliot

The difficult truth about truth is that it often
requires us to change our perspectives,
attitudes, and rules for living.

Susan Lenzkes

Truth suffers, but never dies.

St. Teresa of Avila

Jesus said to him, "I am the way, the truth, and the life. No one comes to the Father except through Me. If you had known Me, you would have known My Father also; and from now on you know Him and have seen Him."

John 14:6-7 NKJV

I have no greater joy than to hear that my children walk in truth.

3 John 1:4 KJV

A person who does not have the Spirit does not accept the truths that come from the Spirit of God. That person thinks they are foolish and cannot understand them, because they can only be judged to be true by the Spirit. The spiritual person is able to judge all things, but no one can judge him.

1 Corinthians 2:14–15 NCV

TODAY'S TIP:

When you speak the truth and live by God's Truth, you'll be very glad you did!

CHAPTER 9

YOUR TESTIMONY

Therefore, everyone who will acknowledge
Me before men, I will also acknowledge
him before My Father in heaven.
Matthew 10:32 Holman CSB

I t's undeniable: those of us who are Christians should be willing to talk about the things that Christ has done for us. But sometimes, because of our shyness or insecurities, we're afraid to share our experiences. And that's unfortunate.

We live in a world that desperately needs the healing message of Christ Jesus. Every believer, each in his or her own way, bears responsibility for sharing the Good News of our Savior.

How can you share your faith without sounding "holier than thou"? Here are things to remember: 1. Be humble 2. Be sincere 3. Don't be so anxious to talk about your own beliefs that you forget to listen to the other person, and 4. Remember that the life you lead (the way that you demonstrate your faith in action) is usually much more important than the words you speak. So don't just talk like a Christian; behave like one, too.

As a believer in Christ, you know how He has touched your heart and changed your life. Now it's your turn to share the Good News with others. And remember: today is the perfect time to share your testimony because tomorrow may simply be too late.

Theology is an interesting school of thought. The Bible is beautiful literature. Sitting in quiet sanctuary, bathed in the amber light from stained-glass windows, having our jangled nerves soothed by the chords from an organ—all that is inspiring. But to tell you the truth, when we leave the classroom, close the church door, and walk out into the real world, it is the indisputable proof of changed lives that makes us believers.

Gloria Gaither

If you are going to live in peace, you need to embrace in faith the reality that "the LORD is in His holy temple." Embrace it and be silent before Him. You don't need to argue. You don't need to defend God. Simply explain Him as the Word of God explains Him. Then it is the skeptic's responsibility to accept or reject the Word of God. The responsibility is his, not yours. It's between him and God. It's a matter of faith.

Kay Arthur

The following night, the Lord stood by him and said,
"Have courage! For as you have testified about Me
in Jerusalem, so you must also testify in Rome."
Acts 23:11 Holman CSB

...always be ready to give a defense to anyone who asks
you a reason for the hope that is in you.
1 Peter 3:15 Holman CSB

Therefore, we are ambassadors for Christ; certain that
God is appealing through us, we plead on
Christ's behalf, "Be reconciled to God."
2 Corinthians 5:20 Holman CSB

TODAY'S TIP:

What if you're uncomfortable talking about your faith? Remember: you're not giving the State of the Union Address—you're having a conversation. And besides, if you're not sure what to say, a good place to start is by asking questions, not making speeches.

CHAPTER 10

YOUR EXAMPLE

*We have around us many people whose lives tell us
what faith means. So let us run the race that is before
us and never give up. We should remove from our lives
anything that would get in the way and the sin
that so easily holds us back.*

Hebrews 12:1 NCV

Whether we like it or not, all of us are role models. Our friends and family members watch our actions and, as followers of Christ, we are obliged to act accordingly.

What kind of example are you? Are you the kind of woman whose life serves as a genuine example of righteousness? Are you a woman whose behavior serves as a positive role model for your family and friends? Are you the kind of woman whose words and deeds are based upon kindness, faithfulness, and a love for the Lord? If so, you are not only blessed by God, you are also a powerful force for good in a world that desperately needs positive influences such as yours.

Corrie ten Boom advised, "Don't worry about what you do not understand. Worry about what you do understand in the Bible but do not live by." And that's sound advice because our families and friends are watching . . . and so, for that matter, is God.

Among the most joyful people I have known have been some who seem to have had no human reason for joy. The sweet fragrance of Christ has shown through their lives.

Elisabeth Elliot

Each one of us is God's special work of art. Through us, He teaches and inspires, delights and encourages, informs and uplifts all those who view our lives. God, the master artist, is most concerned about expressing Himself—His thoughts and His intentions—through what He paints in our character . . . . [He] wants to paint a beautiful portrait of His Son in and through your life. A painting like no other in all of time.

Joni Eareckson Tada

Let us preach you, Dear Jesus, without preaching, not by words but by our example, by the casting force, the sympathetic influence of what we do, the evident fullness of the love our hearts bear to you. Amen.

Mother Teresa

In every way be an example of doing good deeds.
When you teach, do it with honesty and seriousness.
Titus 2:7 NCV

In everything you do, stay away from complaining
and arguing, so that no one can speak a word of blame
against you. You are to live clean, innocent lives as
children of God in a dark world full of crooked
and perverse people. Let your lives shine
brightly before them.
Philippians 2:14-15 NLT

You are the light that gives light to the world . . . .
In the same way, you should be a light for other people.
Live so that they will see the good things you do
and will praise your Father in heaven.
Matthew 5:14,16 NCV

TODAY'S TIP:

Make your actions consistent with your words.
Parental pronouncements are easy to make but much
harder to live by. But whether you like it or not, you
are almost certainly the most important role model
for your child. Speak and behave accordingly.

THE FOURTH COMMANDMENT:

REMEMBER THE SABBATH

The Fourth Commandment states, "Remember the Sabbath day, to keep it holy. Six days you shall labor and do all your work, but the seventh day is the Sabbath of the Lord your God." During the next four days, take time to consider the way that you and your family observe the holiest day of the week: God's day.

CHAPTER 11

THE SABBATH

*But the hour cometh, and now is, when the true
worshippers shall worship the Father in spirit and in
truth: for the Father seeketh such to worship him.*

John 4:23 KJV

When God gave Moses the Ten Commandments, it became perfectly clear that our Heavenly Father intends for His children to make the Sabbath a holy day, a day for worship, for contemplation, for fellowship, and for rest. Yet we live in a seven-day-a-week world, a world that all too often treats Sunday as a bonus shopping day or a regular workday. But the Lord's day deserves to be respected by those who choose to follow the Son of God.

You and your family members will face powerful temptations, temptations to rush through Sunday services and then get on with "business as usual." The world wants you to make Sunday a time for shopping, a time for working, a time for rushing from place to place with scarcely a moment to spare. But God wants you to make the Sabbath a special day—and that's precisely what you should want for you and your family.

How does your family observe the Lord's day? When church is over, do you treat Sunday like any other day of the week? If so, it's time to think long and hard about your family's schedule and your family's priorities.

Whenever we ignore God's commandments, we pay a price. So if you've been treating Sunday as just another day, it's time to break that habit. When Sunday rolls around, don't try to fill every spare moment. Take time to worship and to rest . . . Father's orders!

It's our privilege to not only raise our hands in worship but also to combine the visible with the invisible in a rising stream of praise and adoration sent directly to our Father.

Shirley Dobson

He wants us to worship authentically because it changes us—he changes us.

Sheila Walsh

Worship and worry cannot live in the same heart; they are mutually exclusive.

Ruth Bell Graham

*God lifted him high and honored him far beyond anyone
or anything, ever, so that all created beings in heaven
and earth, even those long ago dead and buried,
will bow in worship before this Jesus Christ,
and call out in praise that he is the Master of all,
to the glorious honor of God the Father.*

Philippians 2:9-11 MSG

*Worship the Lord with gladness. Come before him,
singing with joy. Acknowledge that the Lord is God!
He made us, and we are his. We are his people,
the sheep of his pasture.*

Psalm 100:2-3 NLT

*A time is coming and has now come when the true
worshipers will worship the Father in spirit and truth,
for they are the kind of worshipers the Father seeks.
God is spirit, and his worshipers must
worship in spirit and in truth.*

John 4:23-24 NIV

TODAY'S TIP:

Worship reminds you of the awesome power of God.
So worship Him daily, and allow Him to work through
you every day of the week (not just on Sunday).

CHAPTER 12

THE CHURCH

And I also say to you that you are Peter, and on this rock I will build My church, and the forces of Hades will not overpower it. I will give you the keys of the kingdom of heaven, and whatever you bind on earth will have been bound in heaven, and whatever you loose on earth will have been loosed in heaven.

Matthew 16:18-19 Holman CSB

The Bible teaches that we should worship God in our hearts and in our churches (Acts 20: 28). We have clear instructions to "feed the church of God" and to worship our Creator in the presence of fellow believers.

We live in a world that is teeming with temptations and distractions—a world where good and evil struggle in a constant battle to win our minds, our hearts, and our souls. Our challenge, of course, is to ensure that we cast our lot on the side of God. One way that we remain faithful to Him is through the practice of regular, purposeful worship with our families. When we worship the Father faithfully and fervently, we are blessed.

A living church gathers its members of all age
groups and says, "Come! In this precious, unique,
'now' time, let's all go hard after God!"

Anne Ortlund

Our churches are meant to be havens where
the caste rules of the world do not apply.

Beth Moore

Churches do not lack great scholars and great
minds. They lack men and women who can
and will be channels of the power of God.

Corrie ten Boom

Every time a new person comes to God, every time
someone's gifts find expression in the fellowship of
believers, every time a family in need is surrounded
by the caring church, the truth is affirmed anew: the
Church triumphant is alive and well!

Gloria Gaither

Now you are the body of Christ,
and members individually.
1 Corinthians 12:27 NKJV

Be on guard for yourselves and for all the flock,
among which the Holy Spirit has made you overseers,
to shepherd the church of God which
He purchased with His own blood.
Acts 20:28 NASB

The church, you see, is not peripheral to the world;
the world is peripheral to the church. The church is
Christ's body, in which he speaks and acts,
by which he fills everything with his presence.
Ephesians 1:23 MSG

TODAY'S TIP:

Make church a celebration, not an obligation: Your attitude towards church is important, in part, because it is contagious . . . so celebrate accordingly!

CHAPTER 13

RENEWAL

When doubts filled my mind,
your comfort gave me renewed hope and cheer.

Psalm 94:19 NLT

God intends that His children lead joyous lives filled with abundance and peace. But sometimes, as all mothers can attest, abundance and peace seem very far away. It is then that we must turn to God for renewal, and when we do, He will restore us.

Have you "tapped in" to the power of God, or are you muddling along under your own power? If you are weary, worried, fretful, or fearful, then it is time to turn to a strength much greater than your own.

The Bible tells us that we can do all things through the power of our risen Savior, Jesus Christ. Our challenge, then, is clear: we must place Christ where He belongs: at the very center of our lives.

Are you tired or troubled? Turn your heart toward God in prayer. Are you weak or worried? Make the time to delve deeply into God's Holy Word. When you do, you'll discover that the Creator of the universe stands ready and able to create a new sense of wonderment and joy in you.

Repentance removes old sins and wrong attitudes,
and it opens the way for the Holy Spirit
to restore our spiritual health.

Shirley Dobson

But while relaxation is one thing, refreshment is
another. We need to drink frequently
and at length from God's fresh springs,
to spend time in the Scripture, time in fellowship
with Him, time worshiping Him.

Ruth Bell Graham

Each of us has something broken in our lives:
a broken promise, a broken dream, a broken
marriage, a broken heart…and we must decide how
we're going to deal with our brokenness. We can
wallow in self-pity or regret, accomplishing nothing
and having no fun or joy in our circumstances; or we
can determine with our will to take a few risks,
get out of our comfort zone, and see what God will
do to bring unexpected delight in our time of need.

Luci Swindoll

*Create in me a pure heart, O God, and renew a
steadfast spirit within me. Do not cast me from your
presence or take your Holy Spirit from me. Restore to
me the joy of your salvation and grant me
a willing spirit, to sustain me.*

Psalm 51:10-12 NIV

*He makes me to lie down in green pastures;
He leads me beside the still waters.
He restores my soul; He leads me in the paths of
righteousness for His name's sake.*

Psalm 23:2–3 NKJV

TODAY'S TIP:

God wants to give you peace, and He wants to renew
your spirit. It's up to you to slow down and give Him
a chance to do so.

CHAPTER 14

REST

Come to me, all you who are weary and burdened,
and I will give you rest. Take my yoke upon you
and learn from me, for I am gentle and humble in heart,
and you will find rest for your souls.
For my yoke is easy and my burden is light.

Matthew 11:28-30 NIV

Even the most energetic Christians can, from time to time, find themselves running on empty. The demands of daily life can drain us of our strength and rob us of the joy that is rightfully ours in Christ. When we find ourselves tired, discouraged, or worse, there is a source from which we can draw the power needed to recharge our spiritual batteries. That source is God.

God expects us to work hard, of course, but He also intends for us to rest. When we fail to take the rest that we need, we do a disservice to ourselves and to our families.

We live in a world that tempts us to stay up late—very late. But too much late-night TV, combined with too little sleep, is a prescription for exhaustion.

Are your physical or spiritual batteries running low? Is your energy on the wane? Are your emotions frayed? If so, it's time to turn your thoughts and your prayers to God. And when you're finished, it's probably time to turn off the lights and go to bed!

Jesus taught us by example to get out of the rat race
and recharge our batteries.

Barbara Johnson

No soul can have rest until it discovers that
created things are empty. When the soul gives up
all for love, so that it can have Him that is all,
then it finds true rest.

Juliana of Norwich

Life is strenuous. See that your clock
does not run down.

Mrs. Charles E. Cowman

If we stay with the Lord, enduring to the end of
His great plan for us, we will enjoy the rest that
results from living in the kingdom of God.

Serita Ann Jakes

I said to myself, "Relax and rest.
God has showered you with blessings."
Psalm 116:7 MSG

I find rest in God; only he gives me hope.
Psalm 62:5 NCV

Full of hope, you'll relax, confident again;
you'll look around, sit back, and take it easy.
Job 11:18 MSG

TODAY'S TIP:

Do whatever it takes to get enough sleep: Burning the candle at both ends isn't fun or smart. So turn off the TV, and go to bed as soon as possible after your children do. They need a good night's sleep, and so, for that matter, do you.

THE FIFTH COMMANDMENT:

HONOR YOUR PARENTS

The Fifth Commandment makes it clear: we must honor our parents. During the next three days, think about your own parents, think about your children, and think about the joys of being a mother.

CHAPTER 15

THANKS, MOM!

Her children rise up and call her blessed.
Proverbs 31:28 NKJV

DEAR MOM,

It's time to honor you. So thanks for the love, the care, the work, the discipline, the wisdom, the support, and the faith. Thanks for being a concerned parent and a worthy example. Thanks for giving life and for teaching it. Thanks for being patient with me, even when you were tired or frustrated—or both. Thanks for changing diapers and wiping away tears. And thanks for being a godly woman, one worthy of our admiration and our love.

You deserve a smile today, Mom, but you deserve so much more. You deserve our family's undying gratitude. And, you deserve God's love, His grace, and His peace. May you enjoy God's blessings always, and may you never, ever forget how much we love you.

SIGNED, YOUR LOVING FAMILY

The mother is and must be,
whether she knows it or not, the greatest, strongest,
and most lasting teacher her children have.

Hannah Whitall Smith

The woman is the heart of the home.

Mother Teresa

There is no influence so powerful
as that of a mother.

Sarah J. Hale

The loveliest masterpiece of the heart of God
is the heart of a mother.

St. Thérèse of Lisieux

*Listen, my son, to your father's instruction
and do not forsake your mother's teaching.*
Proverbs 1:8 NIV

*Then he went down to Nazareth with them and was
obedient to them. But his mother treasured all these
things in her heart. And Jesus grew in wisdom
and stature, and in favor with God and men.*
Luke 2:51 NIV

*For you created my inmost being; you knit me together
in my mother's womb. I praise you because
I am fearfully and wonderfully made . . . .*
Psalm 139:13-14 NIV

TODAY'S TIP:

Hey Mom, how do you treat your parents? If you're lucky enough to have parents who are living, remember that the way you treat them is the way you're training your kids to treat you.

CHAPTER 16

YOUR FAMILY

*You must choose for yourselves
today whom you will serve . . . as for me
and my family, we will serve the Lord.*

Joshua 24:15 NCV

As every mother knows, family life is a mixture of conversations, mediations, irritations, deliberations, commiserations, frustrations, negotiations, and celebrations. In other words, the life of the typical mom is incredibly varied.

Certainly, in the life of every family, there are moments of frustration and disappointment. Lots of them. But, for those who are lucky enough to live in the presence of a close-knit, caring clan, the rewards far outweigh the frustrations.

No family is perfect, and neither is yours. But, despite the inevitable challenges and occasional hurt feelings of family life, your clan is God's gift to you. That little band of men, women, kids, and babies is a priceless treasure on temporary loan from the Father above. Give thanks to the Giver for the gift of family . . . and act accordingly.

It matters that we should be true to one another,
be loyal to what is a family—only a little family in
the great Household, but still a family, with family
love alive in it and action as a living bond.

Amy Carmichael

Money can build or buy a house. Add love to that,
and you have a home. Add God to that, and you
have a temple. You have "a little colony of
the kingdom of heaven."

Anne Ortlund

The miraculous thing about being a family is
that in the last analysis, we are each dependent of
one another and God, woven together by mercy
given and mercy received.

Barbara Johnson

Our Creator, who divided the year into seasons
and the days into mornings and nights, also divided
people into families. He created this gift of
a structure to offer stability and loving security in
the midst of an unstable and insecure world.

Carol Kuykendall

Love must be without hypocrisy. Detest evil; cling to what is good. Show family affection to one another with brotherly love. Outdo one another in showing honor.

Romans 12:9–10 Holman CSB

Their first responsibility is to show godliness at home and repay their parents by taking care of them. This is something that pleases God very much.

1 Timothy 5:4 NLT

Every kingdom divided against itself will be ruined, and every city or household divided against itself will not stand.

Matthew 12:25 NIV

TODAY'S TIP:

Put God first in every aspect of your life. And while you're at it, put Him first in every aspect of your family's life, too.

CHAPTER 17

YOUR CHILDREN

*But when Jesus saw this, He was indignant
and said to them, "Permit the children to come to Me;
do not hinder them; for the kingdom of God belongs
to such as these. Truly I say to you, whoever does not
receive the kingdom of God like a child will not enter it
at all. And He took them in His arms and began
blessing them, laying His hands on them.*

Mark 10:14-16 NASB

As a mother, you are keenly aware that God has entrusted you with a priceless treasure from above: your child. Every child is different, yet every child is similar in this respect: every child is a glorious gift from above—and with that gift comes immense responsibilities.

Thoughtful mothers (like you) understand the critical importance of raising their children with love, with family, with discipline, and with God. By making God a focus in the home, loving mothers offer a priceless legacy to their children—a legacy of hope, a legacy of love, a legacy of wisdom.

Today, let us pray for our children . . . all of them. Let us pray for our own children and for children around the world. Every child is God's child. May we, as concerned mothers, behave—and pray—accordingly.

You have to love your children unselfishly.
That's hard. But it's the only way.

Barbara Bush

The child that never learns to obey his parents
in the home will not obey God
or man out of the home.

Susanna Wesley

Kids are great. They are exciting. Their potential is
simply phenomenal. And in any given family there
is the potential to change the world for God.

Maxine Hancock

Children are better believers than grown-ups,
and better theologians than many academicians.

Madeleine L'Engle

Train a child in the way he should go,
and when he is old he will not turn from it.
Proverbs 22:6 NIV

I have no greater joy than this, to hear of my children
walking in the truth.
3 John 1:4 NASB

Fix these words of mine in your hearts and minds.
Teach them to your children, talking about them when
you sit at home and when you walk along the road,
when you lie down and when you get up.
Deuteronomy 11:18-19 NIV

TODAY'S TIP:
Taking care of children is demanding, time-consuming, energy-depleting . . . and profoundly rewarding. Don't ever overlook the rewards.

THE SIXTH COMMANDMENT:

YOU SHALL NOT MURDER

The Sixth Commandment warns against murder, but in the New Testament, Jesus goes further. He states, "You have heard that the law of Moses says, 'Do not murder. If you commit murder, you are subject to judgment.' But I say, if you are angry with someone, you are subject to judgment!" (Matthew 5:21 NLT). During the next three days, think about the destructive power of anger and the healing power of love.

CHAPTER 18

LOVE

Anyone who hates a brother or sister is a murderer,
and you know very well that eternal life
and murder don't go together.
1 John 3:15 MSG

Love is a choice. Either you choose to behave lovingly toward others . . . or not; either you behave yourself in ways that enhance your relationships . . . or not. But make no mistake: genuine love requires effort. Simply put, if you wish to build lasting relationships, you must be willing to do your part.

Since the days of Adam and Eve, God has allowed His children to make choices for themselves, and so it is with you. As you interact with family and friends, you have choices to make . . . lots of them. If you choose wisely, you'll be rewarded; if you choose unwisely, you'll bear the consequences.

God does not intend for you to experience mediocre relationships; He created you for far greater things. Building lasting relationships requires compassion, wisdom, empathy, kindness, courtesy, and forgiveness (lots of forgiveness). If that sounds a lot like work, it is—which is perfectly fine with God. Why? Because He knows that you are capable of doing that work, and because He knows that the fruits of your labors will enrich the lives of your loved ones and the lives of generations yet unborn.

Love is a Commandment. It is a choice,
a preference. If we love God with our whole hearts,
how much heart have we left? If we love with our
whole mind and soul and strength, how much
mind and soul and strength do we have left?
We must live this life now.

Dorothy Day

Line by line, moment by moment, special times are
etched into our memories in the permanent ink of
everlasting love in our relationships.

Gloria Gaither

What we have once enjoyed we can never lose. All
whom we love deeply become a part of us.

Helen Keller

Love is extravagant in the price it is willing to pay,
the time it is willing to give, the hardships it is
willing to endure, and the strength it is willing to
spend. Love never thinks in terms of "how little,"
but always in terms of "how much."
Love gives, love knows, and love lasts.

Joni Eareckson Tada

He who says he is in the light, and hates his brother,
is in darkness until now.
1 John 2:9 NKJV

If someone says, "I love God," and hates his brother,
he is a liar; for he who does not love his brother whom he
has seen, how can he love God whom he has not seen?
1 John 4:20 NKJV

But I say unto you, Love your enemies, bless them that
curse you, do good to them that hate you, and pray for
them which despitefully use you, and persecute you;
that ye may be the children of your Father which is in
heaven: for he maketh his sun to rise on the evil and on
the good, and sendeth rain on the just and on the unjust.
For if ye love them which love you, what reward have
ye? do not even the publicans the same?
Matthew 5:44-46 KJV

TODAY'S TIP:
God loves you, and He wants you to reflect His love
to those around you.

CHAPTER 19

FORGIVENESS

*For if you forgive men when they sin against you,
your heavenly Father will also forgive you.
But if you do not forgive men their sins,
your Father will not forgive your sins.*

Matthew 6:14-15 NIV

E ven the most mild-mannered moms will, on occasion, have reason to become angry with the inevitable shortcomings of family members and friends. But wise women are quick to forgive others, just as God has forgiven them.

Forgiveness is God's commandment, but oh how difficult a commandment it can be to follow. Being frail, fallible, imperfect human beings, we are quick to anger, quick to blame, slow to forgive, and even slower to forget. No matter. Even when forgiveness is difficult, God's Word is clear.

If, in your heart, you hold bitterness against even a single person, forgive. If there exists even one person, alive or dead, whom you have not forgiven, follow God's commandment and His will for your life: forgive. If you are embittered against yourself for some past mistake or shortcoming, forgive. Then, to the best of your abilities, forget, and move on. Bitterness and regret are not part of God's plan for your life. Forgiveness is.

Forgiveness is actually the best revenge
because it not only sets us free from the person
we forgive, but it frees us to move into all
that God has in store for us.

Stormie Omartian

God has been very gracious to me,
for I never dwell upon anything wrong which a
person has done to me, as to remember it
afterwards. If I do remember it, I always see
some other virtue in the person.

St. Teresa of Avila

I believe that forgiveness can become a continuing
cycle: because God forgives us, we're to forgive
others; because we forgive others, God forgives us.
Scripture presents both parts of the cycle.

Shirley Dobson

Have you thought that your willingness to
forgive is really your affirmation of
the power of God to do you good?

Paula Rinehart

*If you forgive those who sin against you, your heavenly
Father will forgive you. But if you refuse to forgive
others, your Father will not forgive your sins.*
Matthew 6:14-15 NLT

*And be ye kind one to another, tenderhearted,
forgiving one another, even as God for
Christ's sake hath forgiven you.*
Ephesians 4:32 KJV

*Whenever you stand praying, forgive, if you have
anything against anyone, so that your Father in heaven
will also forgive you your transgressions.*
Mark 11:25 NASB

TODAY'S TIP:
Face facts: forgiveness can be a very hard thing to do.
No matter. God instructs us to forgive others (and to
keep forgiving them), period.

CHAPTER 20

JUDGING OTHERS

Stop judging others, and you will not be judged.
Stop criticizing others, or it will all come back on you.
If you forgive others, you will be forgiven.

Luke 6:37 NLT

We have all fallen short of God's commandments, and He has forgiven us. We, too, must forgive others. And, we must refrain from judging them.

Are you one of those people who finds it easy to judge others? If so, it's time to change.

God does not need (or, for that matter, want) your help. Why? Because God is perfectly capable of judging the human heart . . . while you are not.

As Christians, we are warned that to judge others is to invite fearful consequences: to the extent we judge others, so, too, will we be judged by God. Let us refrain, then, from judging our neighbors. Instead, let us forgive them and love them in the same way that God has forgiven us.

Judging draws the judgment of others.

Catherine Marshall

Perhaps the greatest blessing that religious
inheritance can bestow is an open mind,
one that can listen without judging.

Kathleen Norris

Only Christ can free us from the prison of legalism,
and then only if we are willing to be freed.

Madeleine L'Engle

Don't judge other people more harshly
than you want God to judge you.

Marie T. Freeman

*Why do you look at the speck in your brother's eye,
but don't notice the log in your own eye? Or how can
you say to your brother, "Let me take the speck out of
your eye," and look, there's a log in your eye?
Hypocrite! First take the log out of your eye,
and then you will see clearly to take
the speck out of your brother's eye.*

Matthew 7:3-5 Holman CSB

*You, therefore, have no excuse, you who pass judgment
on someone else, for at whatever point you judge
the other, you are condemning yourself.*

Romans 2:1 NIV

*So when they continued asking him, he lifted up himself,
and said unto them, He that is without sin among you,
let him first cast a stone at her.*

John 8:7 KJV

TODAY'S TIP:

Your ability to judge others requires a divine insight
that you simply don't have. So do everybody
(including yourself) a favor: don't judge.

THE SEVENTH COMMANDMENT:

ADULTERY IS FORBIDDEN

The Seventh Commandment warns against the sin of adultery. And how does Jesus define adultery? Jesus teaches, "You have heard that the law of Moses says, 'Do not commit adultery.' But I say, anyone who even looks at a woman with lust in his eye has already committed adultery with her in his heart" (Matthew 5:27-28 NLT). For the next three days, think about the role that trust plays in all your relationships.

CHAPTER 21

HONESTY AND TRUST

. . . as we have received mercy, we faint not; but have renounced the hidden things of dishonesty, not walking in craftiness, nor handling the word of God deceitfully; but, by manifestation of the truth, commending ourselves to every man's conscience in the sight of God.

2 Corinthians 4:1-2 KJV

The best relationships, and the best marriages, are built upon a foundation of honesty and trust. Without trust, marriages soon begin to wither; with trust, marriages soon begin to flourish.

For Christians, honesty is the right policy because it's God's policy. God's Word makes it clear: "Lying lips are an abomination to the Lord, but those who deal truthfully are His delight" (Proverbs 12:22 NKJV).

Sometimes, honesty is difficult; sometimes, honesty is painful; sometimes, honesty makes us feel uncomfortable. Despite these temporary feelings of discomfort, we must make honesty the hallmark of all our relationships; otherwise, we invite needless suffering into our own lives and into the lives of those we love.

Do you want your love to last forever? Then you and your husband must build a relationship based upon mutual trust and unerring truth. Both of you deserve nothing less . . . and neither, for that matter, does God.

We must learn, then, to relate transparently
and genuinely to others because that is
God's style of relating to us.

Rebecca Manley Pippert

One thing that is important for stable emotional
health is honesty—with self and with others.

Joyce Meyer

The single most important element in any human
relationship is honesty—with oneself,
with God, and with others.

Catherine Marshall

Much guilt arises in the life of the believer
from practicing the chameleon life of
environmental adaptation.

Beth Moore

Therefore laying aside falsehood, speak truth,
each one of you, with his neighbor,
for we are members of one another.
Ephesians 4:25 NASB

But when he, the Spirit of truth, comes,
he will guide you into all truth . . . .
John 16:13 NIV

Jesus answered, "I am the way
and the truth and the life. No one comes
to the Father except through me."
John 14:6 NIV

TODAY'S TIP:

Teach the importance of honesty every day, and, if necessary, use words.

CHAPTER 22

BUILDING BETTER RELATIONSHIPS

Love does no harm to its neighbor.
Therefore love is the fulfillment of the law.
Romans 13:10 NIV

As we travel along life's road, we exchange countless hugs and build lifelong relationships with a small, dear circle of family and friends. And how best do we build and maintain these relationships? Healthy relationships are built upon honesty, compassion, responsible behavior, trust, and optimism. Healthy relationships are built upon the Golden Rule. Healthy relationships are built upon sharing and caring.

Are you the kind of woman who spends the time and the energy required to build strong, healthy, lasting relationships? Barbara Bush had this advice: "Cherish your human connections—your relationships with friends and family." And that's wise counsel because you are blessed, you are loved, and you are vitally important to your family and friends—they most certainly need you, and you most certainly need them.

One way or the other, God, who thought up
the family in the first place, has the very best
idea of how to bring sense to the chaos of broken
relationships we see all around us. I really believe
that if I remain still and listen a lot,
He will share some solutions with me
so I can share them with others.

Jill Briscoe

It is my calling to treat every human being with
grace and dignity, to treat every person,
whether encountered in a palace or a gas station,
as a life made in the image of God.

Sheila Walsh

Living life with a consistent spiritual walk deeply
influences those we love most.

Vonette Bright

Thine own friend, and thy father's friend,
forsake not . . . .
Proverbs 27:10 KJV

Carry each other's burdens, and in this way
you will fulfill the law of Christ.
Galatians 6:2 NIV

And be kind to one another, tenderhearted, forgiving one
another, just as God in Christ forgave you.
Ephesians 4:32 NKJV

TODAY'S TIP:

In every relationship, problems have a way of popping up. When they do, it's best to talk about them (and it's not best to "stew" about them). Conversations can prevent conflagrations.

CHAPTER 23

RIGHTEOUSNESS

Blessed are the pure of heart, for they will see God.
Matthew 5:8 NIV

God has given us a guidebook for righteous living called the Holy Bible. It contains thorough instructions which, if followed, lead to fulfillment, righteousness, and salvation. But, if we choose to ignore God's commandments, the results are as predictable as they are tragic.

The Bible instructs us that a righteous life has many components: faith, honesty, generosity, love, kindness, humility, gratitude, and worship, to name but a few. And, if we seek to follow the steps of our Savior, Jesus Christ, we must, to the best of our abilities, live according to the principles contained in God's Holy Word.

As a loving mother, you are keenly aware that God has entrusted you with a profound responsibility: caring for the needs of your family, including their spiritual needs. To fulfill that responsibility, you must study God's Word and live by it. When you do, your example will be a blessing not only to your loved ones, but also to generations yet to come.

We are in desperate need for women of faith
who are willing to courageously stand against
sin and stand for righteousness.

Susan Hunt

Peace comes only when we acknowledge
that human effort cannot sustain righteousness
any more than it could create it.

Susan Lenzkes

Our progress in holiness depends on God
and ourselves—on God's grace and on
our will to be holy.

Mother Teresa

Holiness is not God's asking us to be "good";
it is an invitation to be "His."

Lisa Bevere

But seek first his kingdom and his righteousness,
and all these things will be given to you as well.

Matthew 6:33 NIV

The Lord will not reject his people;
he will not abandon his own special possession.
Judgement will come again for the righteous,
and those who are upright will have a reward.

Psalm 94:14-15 NLT

The righteous shall flourish like the palm tree:
he shall grow like a cedar in Lebanon.

Psalm 92:12 KJV

TODAY'S TIP:
Avoid people and places that might tempt you to disobey God's commandments.

THE EIGHTH COMMANDMENT:

DO NOT STEAL

The Eighth Commandment offers this straightforward instruction: "You shall not steal." For the next three days, think about the need to work diligently for the things you desire. And think about the need to share the fruits of your labors.

CHAPTER 24

WORK

In all the work you are doing, work the best you can.
Work as if you were doing it for the Lord, not for people.

Colossians 3:23 NCV

Providing for a family requires work, and lots of it. And whether or not your work carries you outside the home, your good works have earned the gratitude of your loved ones and the praise of your Heavenly Father.

It has been said that there are no shortcuts to any place worth going. Mothers agree. Making the grade in today's competitive workplace is not easy. In fact, it can be very difficult indeed. The same can be said for the important work that occurs within the four walls of your home.

God did not create you and your family for lives of mediocrity; He created you for far greater things. Accomplishing God's work is seldom easy. What's required is determination, persistence, patience, and discipline—which is perfectly fine with God. After all, He knows that you're up to the task, and He has big plans for all of you. Very big plans . . .

I long to accomplish a great and noble task,
but it is my chief duty to accomplish small tasks
as if they were great and noble.

Helen Keller

All work, if offered to Him, is transformed.
It is not secular but sacred, sanctified
in the glad offering.

Elisabeth Elliot

Great relief and satisfaction can come from seeking
God's priorities for us in each season, discerning
what is "best" in the midst of many
noble opportunities, and pouring our
most excellent energies into those things.

Beth Moore

Those who have had to wait and work for
happiness seem to enjoy it more, because they
never take it for granted.

Barbara Johnson

*Be strong and brave, and do the work. Don't be afraid
or discouraged, because the Lord God, my God,
is with you. He will not fail you or leave you.*

1 Chronicles 28:20 NCV

*But thanks be to God, who gives us the victory
through our Lord Jesus Christ. Therefore, my beloved
brethren, be steadfast, immovable, always
abounding in the work of the Lord, knowing that
your labor is not in vain in the Lord.*

1 Corinthians 15:57-58 NKJV

. . . each will be rewarded according to his own labor.

1 Corinthians 3:8 NIV

TODAY'S TIP:

Here's a time-tested formula for success: have faith
in God and do the work. Hard work is not simply a
proven way to get ahead; it's also part of God's plan
for all His children (including you).

CHAPTER 25

GENEROSITY

*God has given gifts to each of you from his great variety
of spiritual gifts. Manage them well so that God's
generosity can flow through you.*

1 Peter 4:10 NLT

The thread of generosity is woven—completely and inextricably—into the very fabric of Christ's teachings. As He sent His disciples out to heal the sick and spread God's message of salvation, Jesus offered this guiding principle: "Freely you have received, freely give" (Matthew 10:8 NIV). The principle still applies. If we are to be disciples of Christ, we must give freely of our time, our possessions, and our love.

Lisa Whelchel spoke for Christian women everywhere when she observed, "The Lord has abundantly blessed me all of my life. I'm not trying to pay Him back for all of His wonderful gifts; I just realize that He gave them to me to give away." All of us have been blessed, and all of us are called to share those blessings without reservation.

Today, make this pledge and keep it: Be a cheerful, generous, courageous giver. The world needs your help, and you need the spiritual rewards that will be yours when you share your possessions, your talents, and your time.

The Christian gives all she knows of herself
to all she knows of God and continues
to grow in the knowledge of both.

Gladys Hunt

As faithful stewards of what we have,
ought we not to give earnest thought
to our staggering surplus?

Elisabeth Elliot

The measure of a life, after all,
is not its duration but its donation.

Corrie ten Boom

A cup that is already full cannot have more added
to it. In order to receive the further good
to which we are entitled, we must give
of that which we have.

Margaret Becker

*Now this I say, he who sows sparingly will also reap
sparingly, and he who sows bountifully will also reap
bountifully. Each one must do just as he has purposed in
his heart, not grudgingly or under compulsion,
for God loves a cheerful giver.*

2 Corinthians 9:6-7 NASB

*In every way I've shown you that by laboring like this,
it is necessary to help the weak and to keep in mind the
words of the Lord Jesus, for He said,
"It is more blessed to give than to receive."*

Acts 20:35 Holman CSB

*Be generous: Invest in acts of charity.
Charity yields high returns.*

Ecclesiastes 11:1 MSG

TODAY'S TIP:

Teaching generosity: It's never too early to emphasize
the importance of giving. From the time that a child
is old enough to drop a penny into the offering plate,
we, as parents, should stress the obligation that we
all have to share the blessings that God has shared
with us.

CHAPTER 26

SERVING OTHERS

*But whosoever will be great among you, let him be
your minister; and whosoever will be chief among you,
let him be your servant: even as the Son of man came
not to be ministered unto, but to minister,
and to give his life a ransom for many.*

Matthew 20:26-28 KJV

We live in a world that glorifies power, prestige, fame, and money. But the words of Jesus teach us that the most esteemed men and women in this world are not the self-congratulatory leaders of society but are instead the humblest of servants.

Today, you may feel the temptation to build yourself up in the eyes of your neighbors. Resist that temptation. Instead, serve your neighbors quietly and without fanfare. Find a need and fill it . . . humbly. Lend a helping hand . . . anonymously. Share a word of kindness . . . with quiet sincerity. As you go about your daily activities, remember that the Savior of all humanity made Himself a servant, and we, as His followers, must do no less.

I have discovered that when I please Christ,
I end up inadvertently serving others
far more effectively.

Beth Moore

In serving we uncover the greatest fulfillment
within and become a stellar example of
a woman who knows and loves Jesus.

Vonette Bright

A woman after God's own heart is a woman who
carefully cultivates a servant's spirit.

Elizabeth George

We'll know how to lovingly serve others as we trust
him to give us the guidance we need.

Sheila Cragg

The greatest among you will be your servant.
For whoever exalts himself will be humbled,
and whoever humbles himself will be exalted.
Matthew 23:11-12 NIV

Each of you should look not only to your own interests,
but also to the interest of others.
Philippians 2:4 NIV

A generous man will prosper; he who refreshes others
will himself be refreshed.
Proverbs 11:25 NIV

TODAY'S TIP:

Jesus modeled servanthood. Follow His example, even when service to others requires sacrifice on your part.

THE NINTH COMMANDMENT:

DO NOT BEAR FALSE WITNESS

The Ninth Commandment offers this warning: "You shall not bear false witness against your neighbor." During the next three days, think about the importance of the words you speak.

CHAPTER 27

SPEECH

*Be gracious in your speech. The goal is to bring out
the best in others in a conversation,
not put them down, not cut them out.*

Colossians 4:6 MSG

The words that we speak have great power. If our words are encouraging, we can lift others up; if our words are hurtful, we can hold others back. The Bible reminds us that "Reckless words pierce like a sword, but the tongue of the wise brings healing" (Proverbs 12:18 NIV). In other words, if we are to solve more problems than we start, we must measure our words carefully.

Sometimes, even the most thoughtful among us speak first and think second (with decidedly mixed results). A far better strategy, of course, is to do the more difficult thing: to think first and to speak next.

Do you seek to be a worthy ambassador for Christ? If so, you must speak words that are worthy of your Savior. So avoid angry outbursts. Refrain from impulsive outpourings. Terminate tantrums. Instead, speak words of encouragement and hope to a world that desperately needs both.

The battle of the tongue is won not in the mouth,
but in the heart.

Annie Chapman

A little kindly advice is better than
a great deal of scolding.

Fanny Crosby

Every word we speak, every action we take,
has an effect on the totality of humanity.
No one can escape that privilege—
or that responsibility.

Laurie Beth Jones

When you talk, choose the very same words that
you would use if Jesus were looking over
your shoulder. Because He is.

Marie T. Freeman

*Watch the way you talk. Let nothing foul
or dirty come out of your mouth.
Say only what helps, each word a gift.*

Ephesians 4:29 MSG

*If anyone considers himself religious and
yet does not keep a tight rein on his tongue,
he deceives himself and his religion is worthless.*

James 1:26 NIV

TODAY'S TIP:

Parents set the boundaries: Whether they realize it
or not, parents (not kids) establish the general tone
of the conversations that occur within their homes.
And it's up to parents to ensure that the tone of those
conversations is a tone that's pleasing to God.

CHAPTER 28

WORDS

To everything there is a season . . .
a time to keep silence, and a time to speak.
Ecclesiastes 3:1,7 KJV

This world can be a difficult place, a place where many of our friends and family members are troubled by the inevitable challenges of everyday life. And since we can never be certain who needs our help, we should be careful to speak helpful words to everybody who crosses our path.

In the book of Ephesians, Paul writes, "Do not let any unwholesome talk come out of your mouths, but only what is helpful for building others up according to their needs, that it may benefit those who listen" (4:29 NIV). Paul reminds us that when we choose our words carefully, we can have a powerful impact on those around us.

Today, let's share kind words, smiles, encouragement, and hugs with family, with friends, and with the world.

We do have the ability to encourage or
discourage each other with the words we say.
In order to maintain a positive mood,
our hearts must be in good condition.

Annie Chapman

Words. Do you fully understand their power?
Can any of us really grasp the mighty force behind
the things we say? Do we stop and think before we
speak, considering the potency of
the words we utter?

Joni Eareckson Tada

Attitude and the spirit in which we communicate
are as important as the words we say.

Charles Stanley

For out of the overflow of the heart the mouth speaks.
Matthew 12:34 NIV

*But I say unto you, That every idle word that men
shall speak, they shall give account thereof in the day of
judgment. For by thy words thou shalt be justified,
and by thy words thou shalt be condemned.*
Matthew 12:36-37 KJV

*Reckless words pierce like a sword,
but the tongue of the wise brings healing.*
Proverbs 12:18 NIV

TODAY'S TIP:
Words, words, words . . . are important, important,
important! And, some of the most important words
you will ever speak are the ones that your children
hear. So whether or not you are talking directly to
your kids, choose your words carefully.

CHAPTER 29

ENCOURAGEMENT

Let's see how inventive we can be in encouraging love and helping out, not avoiding worshipping together as some do but spurring each other on.

Hebrews 10:24-25 MSG

Every member of your family needs a regular supply of encouraging words and pats on the back. And you need the rewards that God gives to enthusiastic moms who are a continual source of encouragement to their families.

As Christians, we are instructed to choose our words carefully so as to build others up through wholesome, honest encouragement. How can we build others up? By celebrating their victories and their accomplishments. As the old saying goes, "When someone does something good, applaud—you'll make two people happy."

Today, look for the good in others—starting with your family. And then, celebrate the good that you find. When you do, you'll be a powerful force of encouragement in your corner of the world . . . and a worthy servant to your God.

Encouragement is to a friendship
what confetti is to a party.

Nicole Johnson

If someone listens or stretches out a hand or
whispers a word of encouragement or
attempts to understand a lonely person,
extraordinary things begin to happen.

Loretta Girzartis

Giving encouragement to others is a most welcome
gift, for the results of it are lifted spirits,
increased self-worth, and a hopeful future.

Florence Littauer

My special friends, who know me so well
and love me anyway,
give me daily encouragement to keep on.

Emilie Barnes

Watch the way you talk. Let nothing foul
or dirty come out of your mouth.
Say only what helps, each word a gift.
Ephesians 4:29 MSG

Encourage each other. Live in harmony and peace.
Then the God of love and peace will be with you.
2 Corinthians 13:11 NLT

Let the word of Christ dwell in you richly in all wisdom;
teaching and admonishing one another in psalms
and hymns and spiritual songs,
singing with grace in your hearts to the Lord.
Colossians 3:16 KJV

TODAY'S TIP:
Understand that your words have immense power to
encourage or discourage others.

THE TENTH COMMANDMENT:

DON'T COVET

The Tenth Commandment warns: "You shall not covet." During the next two days, consider the negative impact that envy can have upon your life.

CHAPTER 30

BEYOND ENVY

*So rid yourselves of all wickedness, all deceit,
hypocrisy, envy, and all slander.*
1 Peter 2:1 Holman CSB

Because we are frail, imperfect human beings, we are sometimes envious of others. But God's Word warns us that envy is sin. Thus, we must guard ourselves against the natural tendency to feel resentment and jealousy when other people experience good fortune.

As believers, we have absolutely no reason to be envious of any people on earth. After all, as Christians we are already recipients of the greatest gift in all creation: God's grace. We have been promised the gift of eternal life through God's only begotten Son, and we must count that gift as our most precious possession.

Rather than succumbing to the sin of envy, we should focus on the marvelous things that God has done for us—starting with Christ's sacrifice. And we must refrain from preoccupying ourselves with the blessings that God has chosen to give others.

So here's a surefire formula for a happier, healthier life: Count your own blessings and let your neighbors count theirs. It's the godly way to live.

Discontent dries up the soul.

Elisabeth Elliot

What God asks, does, or requires of others
is not my business; it is His.

Kay Arthur

How can you possess the miseries of envy
when you possess in Christ the best of all portions?

C. H. Spurgeon

Do not covet your neighbor's house . . .
or anything that belongs to your neighbor.
Exodus 20:17 Holman CSB

We must not become conceited, provoking
one another, envying one another.
Galatians 5:26 Holman CSB

For where envy and selfish ambition exist,
there is disorder and every kind of evil.
James 3:16 Holman CSB

TODAY'S TIP:
Feelings of envy will rob you of happiness and peace.
Don't allow yourself to be robbed.

CHAPTER 31

LASTING CONTENTMENT

But godliness with contentment is great gain.
For we brought nothing into the world, and we can
take nothing out of it. But if we have food and clothing,
we will be content with that.

1 Timothy 6:6-8 NIV

The preoccupation with happiness and contentment is an ever-present theme in the modern world. We are bombarded with messages that tell us where to find peace and pleasure in a world that worships materialism and wealth. But, lasting contentment is not found in material possessions; genuine contentment is a spiritual gift from God to those who trust in Him and follow His commandments.

Where can you and your family members find contentment? If you don't find it in God, you will never find it anywhere else. But, if you put your faith and your trust in Him, you will be blessed with an inner peace that is beyond human understanding. When God dwells at the center of your lives, peace and contentment will belong to you just as surely as you belong to God.

When you accept rather than fight your
circumstances, even though you don't understand
them, you open your heart's gate to God's love,
peace, joy, and contentment.

Amy Carmichael

When we do what is right, we have contentment,
peace, and happiness.

Beverly LaHaye

Those who are God's without reserve are,
in every sense, content.

Hannah Whitall Smith

The key to contentment is to consider.
Consider who you are and be satisfied with that.
Consider what you have and be satisfied with that.
Consider what God's doing and be
satisfied with that.

Luci Swindoll

*Keep your lives free from the love of money and be
content with what you have, because God has said,
"Never will I leave you; never will I forsake you."*

Hebrews 13:5 NIV

*I have learned, in whatsoever state I am,
therewith to be content.*

Philippians 4:11 KJV

*I know what it is to be in need, and I know what it is to
have plenty. I have learned the secret of being content
in any and every situation, whether well fed
or hungry, whether living in plenty or in want.
I can do everything through him who gives me strength.*

Philippians 4:12-13 NIV

TODAY'S TIP:

Contentment comes not from your circumstances,
but from your attitude. And remember this: peace
with God is the foundation of a contented life.